The Pacific Ocean

by Anne Ylvisaker

Consultant:
Sarah E. Schoedinger
Education Coordinator
Consortium for Oceanographic Research and Education
Washington, D.C.

Bridgestone Books
an imprint of Capstone Press
Mankato, Minnesota

Bridgestone Books are published by Capstone Press
151 Good Counsel Drive, P.O. Box 669, Mankato, Minnesota 56002
http://www.capstone-press.com

Library of Congress Cataloging-in-Publication Data
Ylvisaker, Anne.
    The Pacific Ocean / by Anne Ylvisaker.
    p. cm.—(Oceans)
    Includes bibliographical references and index.
    Summary: Introduces the earth's largest ocean, and provides instructions for an
activity to demonstrate how the tropical storms known as typhoons spin.
    ISBN 0-7368-1426-4 (hardcover)
    1. Oceanography—Pacific Ocean—Juvenile literature. [1. Pacific Ocean.
2. Oceanography.] I. Title.
GC771 .Y58 2003
551.46′5—dc21   2001007910

Editorial Credits
Megan Schoeneberger, editor; Karen Risch, product planning editor; Linda Clavel,
        designer; Image Select International, photo researcher

Photo Credits
Art Directors and TRIP/H. Rogers, 12, 14; Corbis/Ralph A. Clevenger, 18; Digital
Wisdom/Mountain High, 6, 8 (map); Erin Scott/SARIN Creative, 10; ImageState,
16, 20; The Naval Historical Center, 8 (photo); PhotoDisc, Inc., cover, 4; RubberBall
Productions, 22, 23

1 2 3 4 5 6 07 06 05 04 03 02

Table of Contents

Fun Fact
The Pacific Ocean is the deepest ocean.

4

The Pacific Ocean

The Pacific Ocean is the largest ocean. It is larger than all of the continents put together. The Pacific covers 60 million square miles (155 million square kilometers). It is about 15 times larger than the United States.

continent
one of the seven main
landmasses of Earth

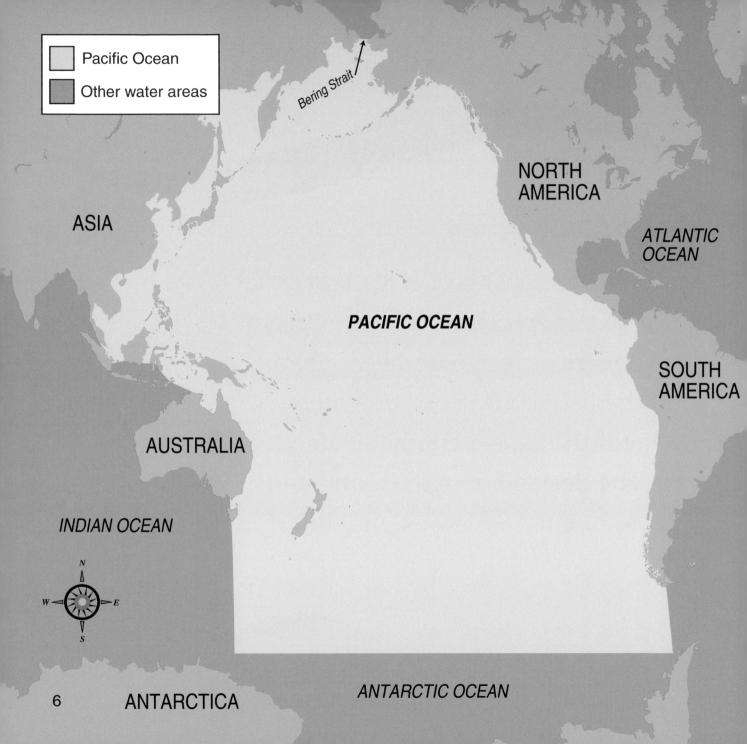

Pacific Ocean

Other water areas

Bering Strait

NORTH
AMERICA

ATLANTIC
OCEAN

ASIA

PACIFIC OCEAN

SOUTH
AMERICA

AUSTRALIA

INDIAN OCEAN

N

W   E

S

6   ANTARCTICA

ANTARCTIC OCEAN

The Location of the Pacific Ocean

Four continents and three oceans border the Pacific Ocean. North America, South America, and the Atlantic Ocean border the Pacific on the east. Asia, Australia, and the Indian Ocean lie to the west. The Bering Strait lies to the north. The Antarctic Ocean is to the south.

strait

a narrow strip of water that connects two larger bodies of water

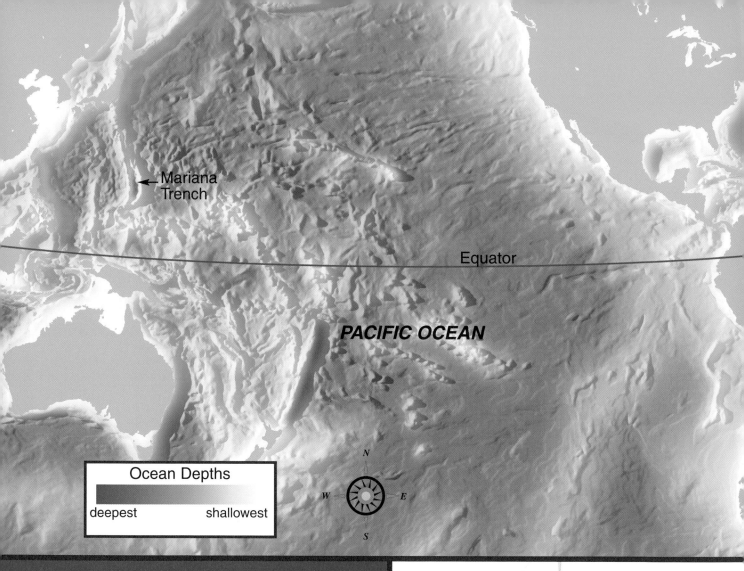

Mariana
Trench ←

Equator

PACIFIC OCEAN

Ocean Depths

deepest   shallowest

N
W   *E*
S

The *Trieste*, shown at right, holds the record for the deepest dive ever made. Two scientists took this underwater machine almost to the bottom of Challenger Deep. The dive took four hours and 48 minutes.

The Depth of the Pacific Ocean

The average depth of the Pacific Ocean is about 14,000 feet (4,300 meters). This depth is about 2.5 miles (4 kilometers). The deepest place in the Pacific is called Challenger Deep. It is in the Mariana Trench. There, the ocean is almost 7 miles (11 kilometers) deep.

depth
a measure of how deep something is

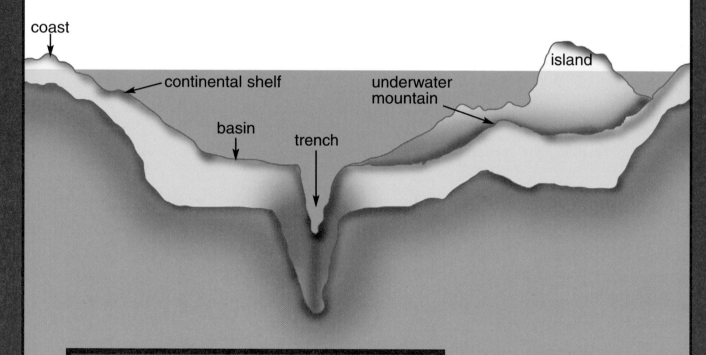

coast

continental shelf

island

underwater mountain

basin

trench

Fun Fact

Scientists think the Pacific Ocean has as many as 1 million underwater volcanoes. A volcano is a mountain with vents. Melted rock flows out of the vents when a volcano erupts.

The Bottom of the Pacific Ocean

The continental shelf is the shallowest part of the ocean floor. It slopes from the coast to the basin. The basin has volcanoes, mountains, and trenches. The East Pacific Rise is an underwater mountain range in the Pacific Ocean.

basin
the low, flat part
of the ocean's floor

Fun Fact
A tsunami (tsoo-NAH-mee) is a very large wave. One of the largest tsunamis reached 1,700 feet (520 meters). It happened in the Pacific Ocean near Alaska in 1958.

The Water in the Pacific Ocean

Salt from soil washes into the Pacific Ocean. This salt makes the water salty. The Pacific is cold in the far north and south. The Pacific is warmest near the equator. There, the surface water temperature reaches 82 degrees Fahrenheit (28 degrees Celsius).

equator
an imaginary line around
the middle of Earth

The Climate around the Pacific Ocean

The climate around the Pacific Ocean is warmest at the equator. Storms form above warm Pacific water. They bring rainfall. Some very strong storms are called typhoons. They cause high winds and large waves. Typhoons lose strength once they reach land.

climate
the usual weather
that occurs in a place

Animals in the Pacific Ocean

Many animals live in the Pacific Ocean. Coral reefs like the Great Barrier Reef in Australia are home to colorful fish. Fish such as tuna and salmon also swim in the Pacific. Sea otters, seals, and whales live in the Pacific. Sea turtles lay eggs on land. They then return to the ocean.

coral reef
an area of coral skeletons
near the surface of the ocean

Plants in the Pacific Ocean

Ocean plants grow in shallow water. Giant kelp can be 125 feet (38 meters) tall. Forests of giant kelp grow near North and South America. They also grow near Australia. Phytoplankton float near the surface of the Pacific. These tiny plants are food for many ocean animals.

kelp
a type of seaweed

Keeping the Pacific Ocean Healthy

People need to keep the Pacific Ocean healthy. Trash left on beaches can kill animals. Oil spills in the Pacific have killed animals and plants. Pollution hurts coral reefs. Many animals in the ocean are endangered because of pollution.

pollution
materials that hurt Earth's water, air, and land

Hands On: Typhoons

Typhoons are storms with very strong winds. Typhoon winds spin clockwise. Try this experiment to see how the winds spin.

What You Need

2-quart (2-liter) bowl
Water
Black pepper
Large spoon

What You Do

1. Fill the bowl more than half full with water.
2. Sprinkle pepper over the top of the water.
3. Stir the water with the spoon in a clockwise direction.
4. Pull the spoon out and watch the pepper continue to swirl.

Notice how the pepper gathers at the center of the bowl. The center is the "eye" of the storm, where the air is calm. The winds of a typhoon spin in a similar way.

Words to Know

average (AV-uh-rij)—the most common amount of something; an average amount is found by adding figures together and dividing by the number of figures.

continental shelf (kon-tuh-NEN-tuhl SHELF)—the shallow area of an ocean's floor near a coast

endangered (en-DAYN-jurd)—at risk of dying out

phytoplankton (FITE-oh-plangk-tuhn)—tiny plants that drift in oceans; phytoplankton are too small to be seen without a microscope.

shallow (SHAL-oh)—not deep

surface (SUR-fiss)—the top or outside layer of something

trench (TRENCH)—a long, narrow valley in an ocean

typhoon (tye-FOON)—a powerful storm with high winds and large waves; typhoons are very much like the hurricanes that happen in the Atlantic Ocean.

Read More

Petersen, David, and Christine Petersen. *The Pacific Ocean.* A True Book. New York: Children's Press, 2001.

Prevost, John F. *Pacific Ocean.* Oceans and Seas. Minneapolis: Abdo, 2000.

Taylor, L. R. (Leighton R.) *The Pacific Ocean.* Life in the Sea. Woodbridge, Conn.: Blackbirch Press, 1998.

Internet Sites

The Biggest Wave—Lituya Bay Tsunami
http://extremescience.com/biggestwave.htm
Oceanlink
http://www.oceanlink.island.net
Virtual Wildlife—Oceans
http://www.panda.org/kids/wildlife/idxocmn.htm

Index